BREXIT

Britain's decision to leave the European Union

Daniel Nunn

Raintree is an imprint of Capstone Global Library Limited, a company incorporated in England and Wales having its registered office at 264 Banbury Road, Oxford OX2 7DY – Registered company number: 6695582

www.raintree.co.uk
myorders@raintree.co.uk

Text © Capstone Global Library Limited 2017
The moral rights of the proprietor have been asserted.

Edited by Helen Cox Cannons
Designed by Philippa Jenkins
Picture research by Morgan Walters
Production by Steve Walker
Originated by Capstone Global Library Ltd
Printed and bound in Great Britain by Ashford Colour Press Ltd

ISBN 978 1 4747 4775 2
20 19 18 17 16
10 9 8 7 6 5 4 3 2 1

British Library Cataloguing in Publication Data
A full catalogue record for this book is available from the British Library.

Acknowledgements
We would like to thank the following for permission to reproduce photographs: Capstone Press: International Mapping Associates, Inc, 7; Shutterstock: 1000 Words, 17, 20, A. C. Hirsch, 24, BasPhoto, 13, Botond Horvath, 9, Charlie Bard, 25, david muscroft, 16, designer491, 5, Drop of Light, 11, Helen Hotson, 28, ImageFlow, 6, Imran's Photography, 18, lazyllama, 4, Mark Yuill, 15, MediaPictures.pl, 12, melis, 23, Michele Paccione, Cover, Monkey Business Images, 10, pathdoc, 30, PomInOz, 14, r.nagy, 19, Thinglass, 29, Twocoms, 26, unverdorben jr, 8, vchal, 27, worradirek, 22.

Every effort has been made to contact copyright holders of material reproduced in this book. Any omissions will be rectified in subsequent printings if notice is given to the publisher.

Contents

Some words are shown in bold, **like this**. You can find out what they mean by looking in the glossary.

A very important decision

On 23 June 2016, the people of the United Kingdom voted in a very important **referendum**. A referendum is held when the **government** wants the people to help them make an important decision. Everyone who votes in a referendum answers the same question.

All voters in the referendum had to fill out a **ballot paper** like this one.

NEWS

BREXIT

referendums however, difficult

The day after the referendum, people woke up to the news that Britain had decided to leave the European Union (EU). This was known as "Brexit".

The big question of the 23 June referendum was: should the United Kingdom remain a member of the European Union or leave the European Union? For months, **campaigners** had tried to persuade voters to choose either to "Remain" or "Leave". Now it was time for the people to decide!

What is the European Union?

The history of the European Union (EU) began in 1957, when six countries decided to work more closely together. These countries were France, West Germany, Italy, Belgium, Luxembourg and the Netherlands. Together they created what was called the European Economic Community (EEC).

The European Union flag is a circle of gold stars on a blue background.

Over the years, more and more countries decided to join the EEC. The United Kingdom joined in 1973. In 1993, the EEC became known as the European Union (EU). Today, the EU has 28 separate member countries. More than 500 million people live in the EU.

The European Union (EU) is a **single market**. This means that people and businesses can buy and sell things within the EU countries without **restrictions**. People who live in EU member countries also have the **right** to live and work in any of the EU countries.

★★★★★★★★★★★★★

Many European countries also share a single **currency**. This is called the Euro. Britain does not use the Euro. It decided to keep the British pound instead.

The MEPs meet at the European Parliament in Strasbourg, France. There are 751 MEPs in total.

The 28 member countries of the EU also share many **laws**. Ideas for new laws and agreements are put forward by the European Commission in Brussels, Belgium. These laws are then voted on by Members of the European Parliament (MEPs). The United Kingdom has 73 MEPs who sit in the European Parliament.

The countries of the European Union (EU) work together in many other ways. They work together when making agreements with countries that do not belong to the EU (such as China and the United States). EU countries also cooperate in matters such as scientific research, education and security. Finally, the EU also works to make sure that all its **citizens** enjoy the same basic **rights**.

The EU has helped scientists from all over Europe to work together.

Sometimes, the leaders of the 28 EU countries get together. They discuss important questions that will affect the future of Europe.

Members of **governments** from all the EU countries meet at the Council of the European Union. Important decisions are made there. Who goes there depends on what is being talked about at the time. For example, if the Council is holding a meeting about farming, the **ministers** for farming from each of the 28 countries go there to talk together.

What were the arguments for staying in the European Union?

In the months before the **referendum**, the two **campaigns** listed the reasons for and against Britain staying in the European Union (EU). The "Vote Remain" campaign was called "Britain Stronger in Europe". The leaders of the Remain campaign included the Prime Minister, David Cameron, and many important politicians and business leaders. The Remain campaign believed that staying in the EU would allow Britain to have its say in the big issues that affect Europe.

David Cameron wanted Britain to remain in the EU.

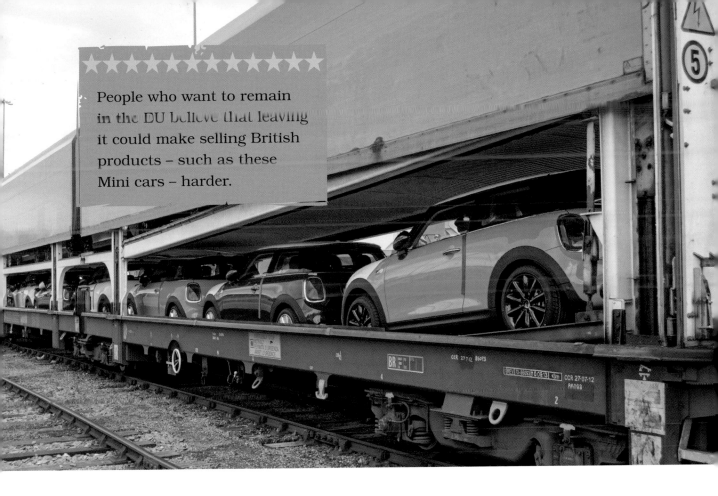

★★★★★★★★★★★★★★★

People who want to remain in the EU believe that leaving it could make selling British products – such as these Mini cars – harder.

One of the main arguments that the Remain campaign gave for staying in the EU was about **trade**. More than 40% of British products sold abroad are sold to EU countries. They argued that leaving the EU could make selling goods into EU countries much more difficult or more expensive. Supporters of the EU say that being a member allows Britain to get better trade deals with non-EU countries, too.

Another reason that the Remain **campaign** gave for staying in the European Union (EU) was **funding**. Britain received EU funding for all sorts of different things. For example, money from the EU has helped to pay for our public transport, farming, building work and science projects.

The European Union has also fought for people's **rights**. This includes important matters such as equal rights for men and women in the workplace.

Money from the EU helped to pay for the Metrolink tram system in Manchester.

An EU **passport** allows the holder to travel freely between all 28 EU member countries.

Another reason that the Remain campaign wanted to remain in the EU was the **freedom of movement**. Through being members of the EU, British people have the right to travel, live and work anywhere within other EU countries. Britain has also **benefited** from people from other European countries living and working in Britain.

What were the arguments for leaving the European Union?

In contrast to the Remain **campaign**, the "Vote Leave" campaign believed that Britain should leave the European Union (EU). The leader of the Leave campaign was Boris Johnson, who is the former Mayor of London. Another well-known supporter of the Leave campaign was Nigel Farage. Farage was the leader of the UK Independence Party (UKIP).

UKIP leader Nigel Farage campaigned for Britain to leave the EU for many years.

Leave **campaigners** believed that leaving the EU would allow Britain to take back control of its borders.

The motto of the Leave campaign was "Take back control". They argued that leaving the EU would allow Britain to reduce the numbers of European people coming to live and work in Britain. They believed that this would mean more jobs for British people and that services such as hospitals and schools would be less crowded.

The Leave **campaign** also believed that leaving the EU would allow Britain to save many millions of pounds' worth of money that currently goes to the EU. Instead of Britain giving that money to the EU, they argued that it could instead be spent on public services such as the National Health Service (NHS), schools and housing.

Vote Leave campaigners said that leaving the EU would free up more money to spend on NHS hospitals like this one.

Leave campaigners wanted more of Britain's laws to be made at the Houses of Parliament in London instead of the European Parliament.

Leave **campaigners** also believed that it would be better for Britain if it could make all of its own **laws**. This was instead of sharing laws with other European countries. Finally, the Vote Leave campaign argued that Britain did not need to be part of the EU to get good **trade** agreements with other countries. They believed that Britain could **negotiate** its own deals with non-EU countries as well as the other EU countries.

23 June 2016: referendum day

The day of the **referendum** was 23 June 2016. **Polling stations** opened at 7 a.m. and closed at 10 p.m. All day, people from all walks of life, old and young, went to polling stations to vote. To be able to vote, you had to be a UK **citizen** over the age of 18. Over 33.5 million people voted one way or the other.

Polling stations were set up in schools, community centres and churches, such as this one.

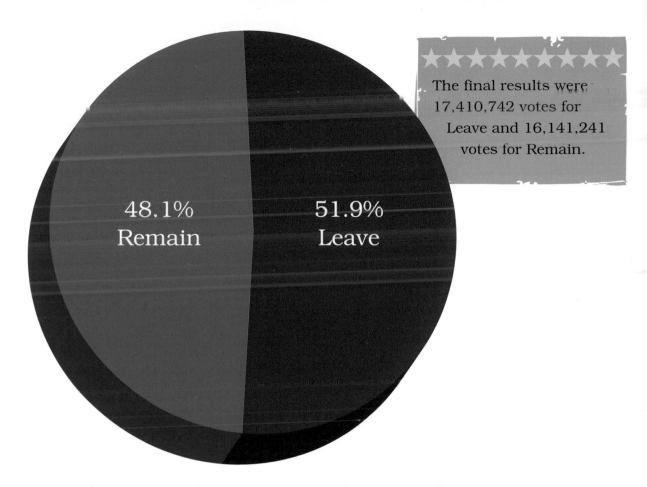

48.1%
Remain

51.9%
Leave

Campaigners on both sides had to wait for the votes to be counted at 382 counting centres around the country. In most places, the vote was incredibly close. At 12.04 a.m., for example, it was announced that 50.7% of people in Newcastle had voted Remain, compared to 49.3% voting Leave. Finally, at around 4 a.m., the national result became clear. By 51.9% to 48.1%, Britain had voted to leave the European Union.

After the vote

In the days following the **referendum**, it became obvious that something huge had happened in Britain's history. The Prime Minister David Cameron **resigned**. This was because he had strongly supported the Vote Remain **campaign**. The value of the British **currency**, the pound, went down dramatically straight away.

In the days after the referendum, it looked like Britain's **economy** was in big trouble.

In the days after the referendum, many people in favour of Remain went on marches to show their support for the EU.

The vote by the British people to leave the European Union (EU) also highlighted the divisions in British society. For those who had voted Leave, the result was a cause for celebration. For people who had voted Remain, however, it was a very sad outcome.

Although 51.9% of voters had voted to leave the European Union (EU), the result was not the same in all parts of the United Kingdom. In Scotland, for example, 62% of people voted Remain. In Northern Ireland, 55.5% voted Remain. This led to lots of discussion about whether Scotland and Northern Ireland may seek independence from the rest of the United Kingdom in order to stay in the EU.

★★★★★★★★★

The **referendum** results were very different in Scotland and Northern Ireland from those of England and Wales.

★★★★★★★★★★★★

Theresa May became Prime Minister in July 2016

Within a few weeks, the situation in Britain began to calm down. The ruling Conservative Party selected a new Prime Minister, Theresa May. She made changes to the **government**. She gave top jobs to people who worked on both the Remain and Leave **campaigns**. Now the task of **negotiating** Britain's exit from the EU would begin.

What happens next?

One of the first decisions made by the new Prime Minister Theresa May was to set up a new **government** office. It is called the Department for Exiting the European Union (EU). The people working there will be in charge of all the **negotiations** with the EU. Nobody knows yet what sort of agreements Britain will be able to make with the EU or how long these might take. No country has ever left the EU before!

The man in charge of the new Department for Exiting the European Union is David Davis. He was one of the leaders of the Leave **campaign**.

Negotiations between Britain and the EU could take a long time to be completed.

There is an agreement called Article 50 of the Lisbon Treaty. According to Article 50, Britain has to officially declare that it wants to leave the EU before the process of leaving can start. Theresa May stated that this process should begin by the end of March 2017. This means that Britain could leave the EU in or around the first half of 2019.

Negotiations will take place on almost every aspect of Britain's relationship with the European Union (EU). The two most difficult issues to talk about are those of **free trade** and **freedom of movement**. Many British businesses want to keep access to the EU's **single market**. This means they would still be able to sell goods across Europe without **restrictions**.

★★★★★★★★★★★

Even **laws** such as where exactly fishing boats from Britain and Europe can fish and how many fish they can catch will need to be agreed upon.

European people living in Britain, such as the owners of this Polish shop in Reading, face uncertain futures.

Many European leaders have warned Britain that it will not be able to keep free trade in the EU unless it continues to allow freedom of movement (the freedom to live and work within any EU country). This is why the issue has become so difficult. Many people voted to leave the EU because they wanted Britain to have more control over who can live and work in Britain.

What do *you* think?

Whatever happens during "Brexit" **negotiations**, things are unlikely to change very much over the next few years. However, the vote to leave the European Union (EU) could change Britain's long-term future. In fact, many people have said that the biggest winners or losers will be the next generation – people who are still at school today!

So, now that you know more about the EU and the arguments to Remain or Leave:
What do *YOU* think?

If you had been allowed to vote in the **referendum**, would you have chosen to Remain or Leave?

Glossary

ballot paper piece of paper used to vote in an election

benefit profit, or do well, from something

campaign organized actions with the aim of achieving a set goal

campaigner person who works in an organized way to achieve a set goal

citizen member of a country who has the right to live there

currency type of money a country uses

economy system in which a country handles its money, property and goods

free trade when a country does not have to pay certain taxes for buying and selling goods from other countries

freedom of movement freedom for a person to live, work and travel around

funding supply of money to be used for a certain purpose

government group of people who make laws, rules and decisions for a country

law rules of a country that must be obeyed

minister member of a government

negotiate discuss something to come to an agreement

negotiations talking to reach an agreement

passport official document that proves a person is a citizen of a certain country and allows them to travel

polling station place where people go to make their vote. This is usually in a public building in a person's local area.

referendum national vote on an important issue

resign give up a job, position or office

restriction limit or control that is placed on someone or something

right something one can or must have by law. People have different rights given to them by the laws of different countries.

single market within the EU, the right to trade between countries without restrictions

trade buying and selling of goods

Find out more

Take a look at these resources to discover more about the European Union (EU):

This book describes each country in the European Union in detail.
The EU Countries, Rob Bowden (Wayland, 2012)

This website from the European Union is packed with information about the EU and its member countries. It also has some games and puzzles.
http://europa.eu/kids-corner/index_en.htm

Index